Get Ready to Giggle!

· JOKE BOOK ·

Library of Congress Control Number 2018950032
ISBN: 978-1-948206-037
www.curiosityinkmedia.com

Manufactured, printed, and assembled in China

Get Ready to Giggle!

· JOKE BOOK ·

by GINA GOLD

Hi, friends!
It's me, Pinkie Pie!

As you know, I'm all about
LAUGHTER! I really, really,
really love making everypony
giggle and guffaw! Whenever
I'm with my Pony Pals Twilight
Sparkle, Rarity, Applejack,
Rainbow Dash, and Fluttershy,
we tell funny jokes to make
each other laugh. Now I
want to share those silly
hoof-slappers with
YOU! So giddy-up,
and get ready to giggle!

Twilight Sparkle was helping Applejack pick apples. Suddenly, a bunch of younger ponies came galloping through the orchard and trampled all the fruit!

Applejack! They've ruined your harvest!

No they didn't. Now I have applesauce!

What does Spike say when he's worn out?

15

What's a pony's favorite state?

Mane!

What do you call the pony who lives next door?

Scootaloo, Apple Bloom, and Sweetie Belle want to have a race for all their pony pals.

Let's call it the Crusader Races! We'll need a track, banners, a timer, and...hmm. What else do we need?

Did you hear about the bitter horse couple?

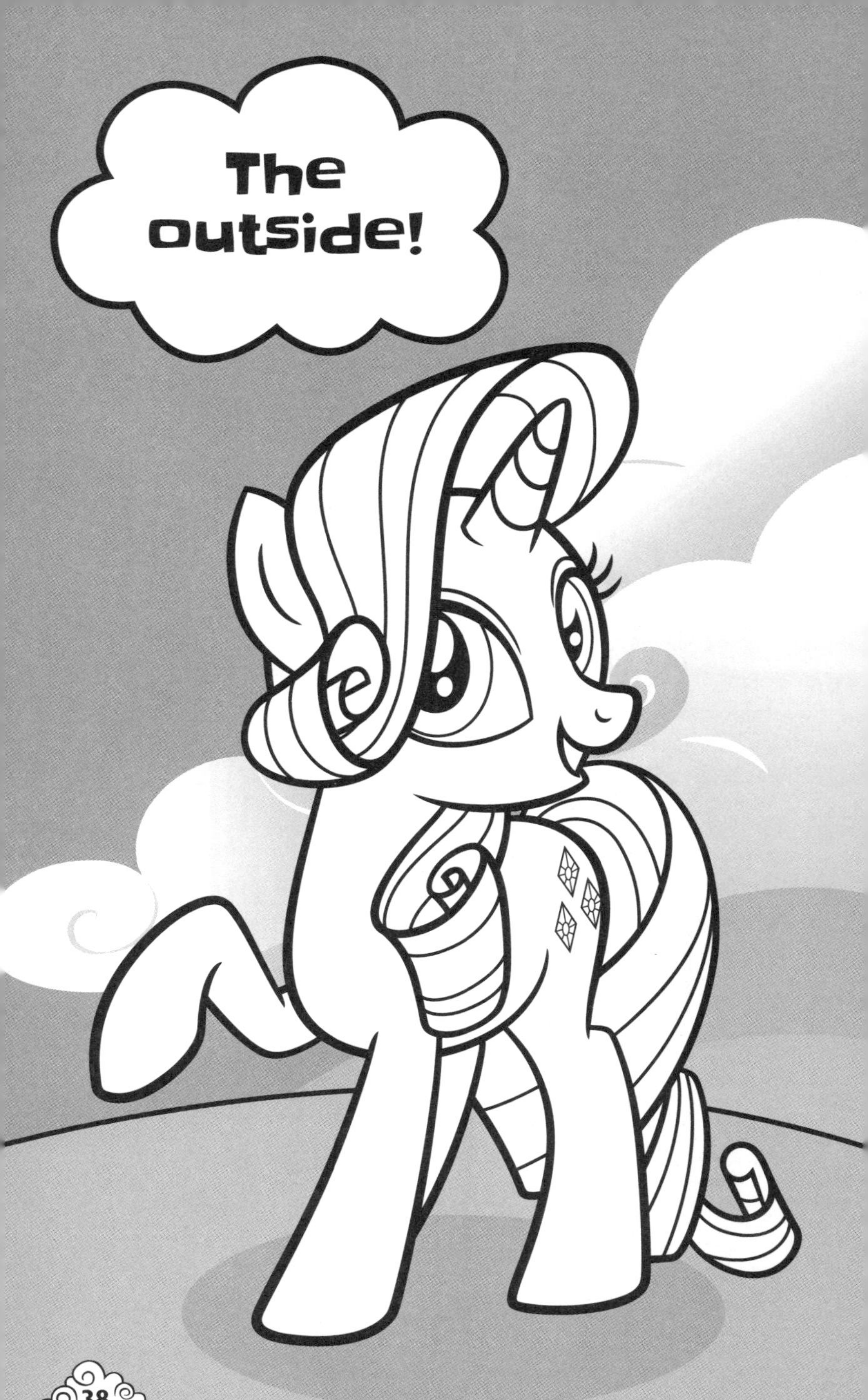
The outside!

A pony, a tomato, and some iceberg lettuce had a race. Guess who won?

The pony.

Because the tomato couldn't *ketchup*, and the lettuce couldn't get a*head*!

41

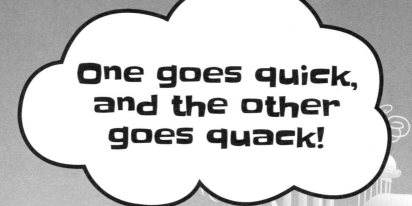

Sweetie Belle told Scootaloo she wanted to join a marching band.

A marching band. Why?

I heard they need horns!

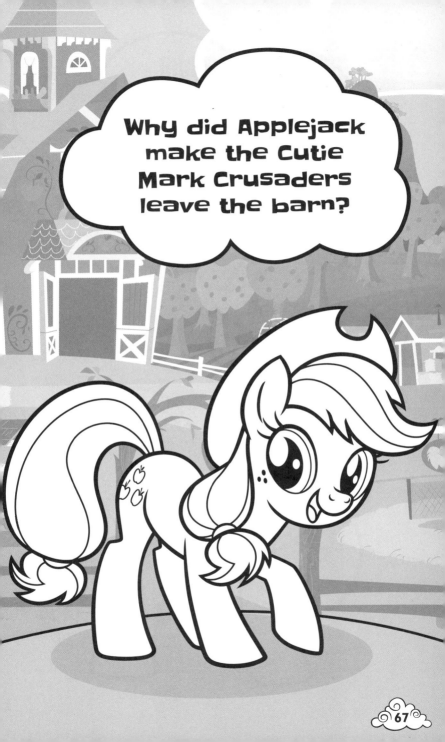

Why did Applejack make the Cutie Mark Crusaders leave the barn?

What time is it when 10 ponies are chasing you?

83

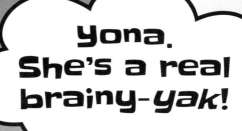

What do you call a pony with a sunburn?

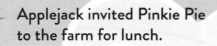

Applejack invited Pinkie Pie to the farm for lunch.